Basic Skil[l]

Cause & Effect

Using Causes and Effects to Make Connections

Grades 3-4

By
Gail Blasser Riley

Cover Illustration by
Laura Zarrin

Published by Instructional Fair • TS Denison
an imprint of

 Children's Publishing

Author: Gail Blasser Riley
Editors: Sara Bierling, Susan Threatt, Meredith Van Zomeren
Cover Illustration: Laura Zarrin
Inside Illustrations: Rebecca Waske

 Children's Publishing

Published by Instructional Fair • TS Denison
An imprint of McGraw-Hill Children's Publishing
Copyright © 2001 McGraw-Hill Children's Publishing

Send all inquiries to:
McGraw-Hill Children's Publishing
3195 Wilson Drive NW
Grand Rapids, Michigan 49544

Cause & Effect—grades 3–4
ISBN: 0-7424-0100-6

5 6 7 8 9 PHXBK 08 07 06 05 04

The McGraw-Hill Companies

About the Book

Cause and Effect for grades 3–4 has been designed to apply a cross-curricular approach to the development of cause and effect skills. Due to the ease of confusing cause and effect with other reading comprehension skills—such as sequencing and predicting—this book has been written with a focus on offering pure cause and effect activities that use clue words such as *why, because, so, since* etc. Additionally, character skills are enhanced as students work through practical life applications to examine consequences of actions through critical thinking.

Students with a wide range of abilities will find this book valuable. Activities are written to guide students carefully, yet challenge them to move forward based on personal ability. Critical thinking skills are fostered all students through cause and effect activities. Students should come away from the book with a renewed respect for their ability to analyze cause and effect in curriculum areas, as well as in their lives outside the classroom.

Table of Contents

...idge to Because

Each picture on the left ...s a cause. Each picture on the right shows an effect.
Draw a bridge f... each cause on the left to its effect on the right.

1.

2.

3.

4.

a.

b.

c.

d.

Bridge to Because (cont.)

> Write two or three sentences explaining how a different cause could result in a different effect.

_____
_____
_____
_____

_____
_____
_____

_____
_____
_____

_____
_____
_____

Camp Days

Tasha couldn't wait to go to camp, but once she got there, she felt a little bit homesick. She sat down to write a letter to her grandmother. Read her letter, then answer the questions on page 7.

Dear Gran,

Thank you for saving up to send me to camp. I love the tennis classes! But I miss the tennis court at the rec center at home. I also miss the tennis matches we always play on Saturday. I miss you, Gran.

The food here is not very good, but the people who sit at my table are really nice. I'd really like to gulp down a frozen yogurt from the corner store near home right about now.

I'm going to ask my friends to take pictures of me tomorrow when we ride our horses. I hardly ever see horses in the city. Getting to ride them is one of the best parts of camp! I wish I could ride horses every day.

I can't wait to see you when camp is over. I know I'll miss my new friends, but I'll write to them a lot.

Love,

Tasha

Camp Days (cont.)

In her letter, Tasha explains things that cause her to like camp and make her want to stay. She also explains why she misses home. Inside the camp cabin, list reasons why Tasha likes camp. List reasons why Tasha misses home inside the apartment building.

TRASH

7

Cause Match

Draw a line from the cause on the left to its effect on the right.

Cause

1. The chain on the bicycle broke.

2. The students worked with chemicals in science class.

3. The computer crashed.

4. The water pipe broke.

5. The dog jumped out of the soapy washtub.

6. The temperature dropped to 30° F (-1° C).

7. The flashbulb on the camera didn't work.

Effect

a. A waterspout shot up out of a manhole.

b. They wore goggles to protect their eyes.

c. Suds splashed all over the porch.

d. The wheels wouldn't turn.

e. The photographs turned out dark.

f. The screen went blank.

g. We could see our breath in the air.

Try this: Think about tasks you do during the day. Write cause and effect matches like the ones above to explain some things you do during the day.

Effect Match

Read the causes inside the rectangle. Draw a line from each cause to an effect outside.

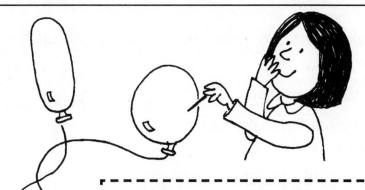

a. It turned green.

b. They became smooth.

c. It broke.

d. The cake burned.

e. They popped.

f. They wouldn't bounce.

g. They wouldn't run.

h. They wilted.

1. The cars ran out of gas.

2. The oven was turned up too high.

3. Water ran across the rocks for many years.

4. He left the heads of lettuce on the counter for two days.

5. She stretched the rubber band too far.

6. Mom touched pins to the balloons.

7. We mixed yellow and blue paint.

8. The basketballs didn't have enough air.

Because, Because, Because

Circle the best ending for each sentence.

1. The weather forecaster predicted a hurricane, so…

   a. we built sandcastles.

   b. the weather forecaster took a vacation.

   c. we went to the hurricane shelter.

2. We ate dinner because…

   a. it was early.

   b. we were hungry.

   c. the mail carrier didn't come.

3. Snow fell all day, so…

   a. the roads were closed.

   b. we swam for hours.

   c. people put away their shovels.

4. I forgot to water the vegetable garden, so…

   a. we had a big crop of tomatoes.

   b. the plants died.

   c. I played all afternoon.

5. The ice cream melted because I…

   a. forgot to put it back in the freezer.

   b. did my homework too fast.

   c. forgot my clarinet.

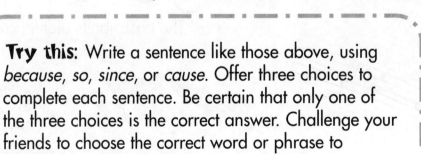

Try this: Write a sentence like those above, using *because, so, since,* or *cause.* Offer three choices to complete each sentence. Be certain that only one of the three choices is the correct answer. Challenge your friends to choose the correct word or phrase to complete each sentence.

Name _____

Step into Effect (cont.)

Creature Feature

Diane loved to play her violin in the orchestra. She loved to watch others dance to her music. Diane knew that people are not the only ones who can create beautiful sounds and joyful dances. Crickets chirp when looking for mates. Scout bees dance when they find lots of food. Diane thought about the joys of the insects as she played *Flight of the Bumblebee* at her recital.

Cause
1. _____
2. _____

Effect
1. Crickets chirp.
2. Scout bees dance.

Now write your own nature paragraph. Tell at least two causes and their effects in your paragraph. Try using words like *because, so, since,* and *cause.* Then fill in the bushes with causes and their effects.

_____

_____
_____
_____
_____

Cause
1. _____
2. _____

Effect
1. _____
2. _____

Name _____

Tell Me Why

Look at each of the following pictures.
Write a sentence to explain the cause and effect in each one.

1.

_____
_____
_____
_____

2.

_____
_____
_____
_____

3.

_____
_____
_____
_____

4.

Draw a picture inside this rectangle that clearly shows a cause and effect.
Challenge a friend to write a cause and effect sentence that describes your picture.

See More about Seas and Lakes

Circle the cause in each sentence. Then draw a line under the effect.

1. Because of oil spills, many sea creatures have died.

2. Ducks have been found with plastic drink rings around their necks because some people have failed to properly dispose of waste.

3. Since turtles are often harmed by traps, many kinds of traps have been outlawed.

4. For protection, lobsters walk in single file when they migrate.

5. A manta ray's gills filter plankton from the water so that the ray can get the food it needs.

6. Because killer whales eat fish and small mammals, they have cone-shaped teeth that help them chew their prey.

7. Because redfish were endangered, fishing for redfish was not permitted.

Try this: Now write your own cause and effect sentence about seas or lakes and the creatures that live in them.

_____

_____

_____

Name _____

Rhyme Climb

> Read the rhymes below. On page 17, you'll find either a cause
> or an effect for each rhyme. If a cause is filled in,
> write the effect. If an effect is filled in, write the cause.

1. Simple Simon met a pieman,
   Going to the fair;
   Says Simple Simon to the pieman,
   Let me taste your ware.
   Says the pieman to Simple Simon.
   Show me first your penny;
   Says Simple Simon to the pieman,
   Indeed I have not any.

2. Hey, diddle, diddle,
   The cat and the fiddle,
   The cow jumped over the moon;
   The little dog laughed
   To see such sport,
   And the dish ran away with the spoon.

3. Little Miss Muffet
   Sat on a tuffet,
   Eating her curds and whey;
   There came a big spider,
   Who sat down beside her
   And frightened Miss Muffet away.

4. Rain, rain, go away,
   Come again another day,
   Little Johnny wants to play.

Rhyme Climb (cont.)

Cause	Effect
1. _____ _____ _____ _____	1. Simple Simon did not get any pie.
2. _____ _____ _____ _____	2. The little dog laughed.
3. A spider sat down beside Miss Muffet.	3. _____ _____ _____ _____
4. Johnny wants to play.	4. _____ _____ _____ _____

Dressing for Dinner

Read the following story. Then complete the activity on page 19.

Will wanted to surprise his dad with a chef's salad for his birthday. He finished the salad, then opened his cookbook to find the recipe for a special salad dressing.

SALAD DRESSING

2 cups oil

1 tablespoon vinegar

1 dash of oregano

1 pinch of salt

Will worked hard to make the salad dressing. He took out a mixing bowl. He measured 2 cups of vinegar and put it in the bowl. He measured 1 tablespoon of oil and put the oil in the mixing bowl. Then he added a dash of oregano and a pinch of salt.

Before Will's dad got home, Will decided to taste the salad. The fresh vegetables made his mouth water. Will put a little bit of salad in a bowl. He scooped salad dressing and drizzled it across the salad. His tongue tingled as he opened his mouth for the first bite. Will gulped. His eyes watered. He couldn't believe the taste in his mouth. He felt prickly points dancing from one side of his mouth to the other. Grabbing a glass of water, Will shook his head. *What did I do wrong?* he wondered.

Dressing for Dinner (cont.)

> Help Will figure out what he did wrong. What can he do to make a tasty salad dressing for his dad? Write a letter to Will giving him the information he needs.

Because I'll Be Responsible

Read the story. Then answer the questions about cause and effect on page 21.

"I want a dog!" Josh said as he stamped his foot on the ground.

"But you didn't take care of your hamster," said his dad, "and we had to give him away."

"This time it will be different. This time I'll take care of my pet. I promise," said Josh.

"I'll think about it," answered Dad.

Josh hung his head and shuffled his feet as he walked to his room.

He looked up at his chores list. Josh knew he had to prove that he was responsible, so he finished all his chores for two weeks, and he finished them in three days!

"Now, Dad, please, can we get a dog? You can see how responsible I've been," Josh pleaded.

Dad smiled. "I think the family down the street still has a few puppies left," he said. "Let's go check them out."

"Hurray!" shouted Josh.

Because I'll Be Responsible (cont.)

1. Why did Josh's dad refuse to let Josh have a dog at first?

_____
_____
_____

2. Why did Josh hang his head?

_____
_____
_____

3. Why did Josh finish all his chores in three days?

_____
_____
_____

4. Why did Josh's dad finally agree to let him have a dog?

_____
_____
_____

Try this: Now write your own cause and effect story. Think about something you have really wanted. What caused you to want it? Did you get it right away? Why or why not? After you write your story, draw a picture to illustrate it.

Proverbial Cause

A proverb is a wise old saying. It contains a hidden or deeper meaning. Explain what you think about the meaning of each of the proverbs on this page and on page 23 by writing a cause and its effect. Use the words *because, so, since,* or *cause* in each of your answers. The first one has been completed for you.

1.

Look before you leap.

<u>You should think before you act because the result may cause problems.</u>

2.

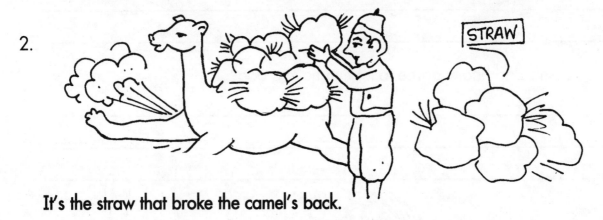

It's the straw that broke the camel's back.

_____

3.

Don't count your chickens before they've hatched.

_____

Proverbial Cause (cont.)

4.

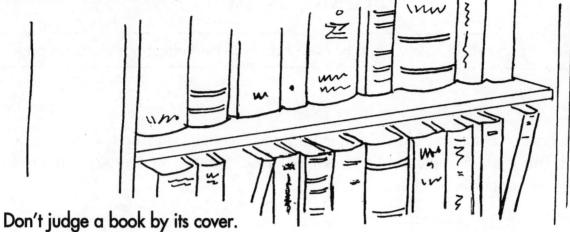

Don't judge a book by its cover.

5.

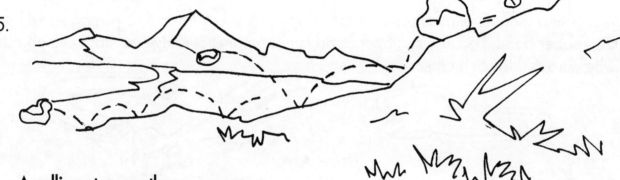

A rolling stone gathers no moss.

6.

Don't cry over spilled milk.

Name _____

Science Action

Read each short article below. Then answer the cause and effect questions on page 25.

Push Off

Fill a balloon with air. Hold the end closed and then let it go. The balloon will zoom forward. This is an example of Newton's third law of motion: for every action, there is an equal and opposite reaction.

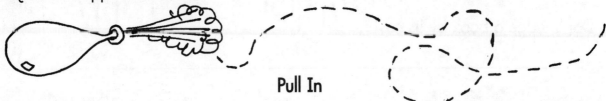

Pull In

Because a magnet attracts some metals, it will pull a key toward it. A magnet will not pull a rubber band, because a rubber band is not magnetic. Only two magnetic objects will be attracted to each other.

Travel Across

Glaciers are large chunks of ice that slowly move over the land. Glaciers have an effect on the land as they travel. Because glaciers pick up parts of the land as they move, glaciers can carve out large areas. And, as glaciers melt, they leave behind bits of earth that can build up areas of land.

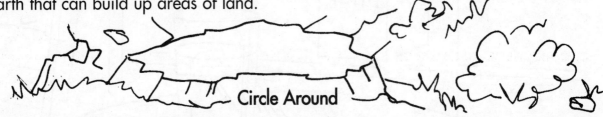

Circle Around

When the sun heats water, the water evaporates and forms vapor. The vapor forms clouds when it cools. The water droplets fall to the earth as rain. The rain evaporates, and the cycle begins again.

Name _____

Science Action (cont.)

> Circle the correct answer for each question below.

1. Glaciers change the land because…

   a. there is an equal and opposite reaction for every action.

   b. water drops grow heavy.

   c. they pick up pieces of land as they move.

   d. they are frozen.

2. If you fill a balloon with air, hold the end, and let it go, it will zoom forward because…

   a. it is frozen.

   b. a balloon is a law of motion.

   c. there is an equal and opposite reaction for every action.

   d. vapor forms clouds.

3. Water evaporates because…

   a. the sun heats up the water.

   b. it is a law of motion.

   c. a magnet attracts metal.

   d. water drops grow heavy.

4. A magnet will pull a key in its direction because…

   a. water drops grow heavy.

   b. the magnet and the key are both magnetic.

   c. a rubber band is not made of metal.

   d. it leaves behind something that has been frozen inside.

Cause Pause

José and his classmates are giving speeches about their favorite vacations, but the microphone in the auditorium is not working quite right. The people in the audience can hear some of the comments, but they cannot hear everything. Help the people in the audience understand what their classmates are saying. Choose the proper phrase from the curtains to complete each speaker's comments.

fell backwards as all the pieces spilled across the floor.

felt a tug at the end of the line.

twisted my ankle.

got a huge blister on my heel.

was as red as a lobster.

1. José: We played on the beach all day, but we forgot our sunscreen, so I...

_____

2. Lu: I skated for hours in my new skates, but there was a hole in my sock, so I...

_____

3. Tia: I used my new fishing rod. I waited for hours. Because I used a good fishing lure, I finally...

_____

4. Ling: I played in a chess tournament. During the third match, someone's dog jumped up on the chess board, and I...

_____

5. Dominique: I ran in six races at camp. Because someone tripped me in the last race, I...

_____

Speaker Squeaker

The microphone in the auditorium is finally fixed, but now the speakers are broken. The people in the audience can hear only a few of their classmates' words. The speakers squeak and squawk. Use the phrases from the curtains to explain each cause.

Mom touched the match to the candle.

1. Lena: I held up my mitt, but I couldn't see the ball.

_____

2. Alfred: Then the flame rose high.

_____

3. Susan: The flowers grew full and tall.

_____

4. Oscar: The wheels turned quickly.

_____

5. Quincy: The soccer ball sailed into the goal.

_____

How the World Wide Web Came to Be

(Read the following article. Then answer the questions below.)

In 1980, scientist Tim Berners-Lee was working with software in the Swiss Alps. He wanted to create a way to organize and find information, so he thought of the World Wide Web.

How did the World Wide Web get its name? Berners-Lee and a coworker tried to think of names. They couldn't come up with ideas they liked. Because they needed a name quickly, they came up with World Wide Web. They planned to think of another name later. However, the name World Wide Web caught on quickly and was never changed.

1. Why did Tim Berners-Lee come up with the idea for the World Wide Web?

_____

_____

_____

2. Why did Tim Berners-Lee and a coworker decide to use the name World Wide Web?

_____

_____

_____

3. Why do you think Tim Berners-Lee thought there needed to be a way to organize and find information?

_____

_____

_____

Out-of-This-World Vacation

(Read the advertisement. Then answer the questions.)

Come join us...

...for a thrilling once-in-a-lifetime vacation! Hop aboard our luxury space liner and fly to the moon for an adventurous six-day vacation. We know you'll love this one because you're thrill-seeking, fun-loving kinds of people. You'll love the happy feeling of floating through the air. And, because there's no gravity, your luggage will feel as light as air. Since we'll be approximately 221,456 miles (356,399 km) above the earth, you'll find the view amazing. We hope you join us for this awesome trip!

Rules and Restrictions:
Due to a decreased amount of fresh air, no smoking will be allowed on the flight. Because of the high risk of travel, all passengers must have life insurance. A charge of $8.4 million will be in place due to high fuel costs.

1. Why does the travel agency know people will love this vacation?

_____

2. Why will travelers' luggage feel as light as air?

_____

3. Why will the view be amazing?

_____

4. Why is no smoking allowed?

_____

5. What must passengers have because of the high risk of travel?

_____

6. Why does the trip cost $8.4 million?

_____

A Grand Debut

Read the story. Then answer the questions.

Keisha loved to watch ballet because the dancers fly through the air. They make great leaps and jumps. One day, Keisha decided she wanted to be a ballerina. So she practiced standing on her toes all day long. Nothing happened. Then she practiced leaping across the living room. Once she even leaped off the couch. Keisha still didn't feel like a ballerina!

Keisha was desperate. She wanted to be a ballerina more than anything else. Finally, she asked her mom to buy her a tutu. Surely that would mean she was a ballerina. She slipped on the tutu and waited. Nothing happened. Keisha sat down on the floor and cried. *Why can't I be a ballerina*, she thought. Just then, Keisha's mom dropped a paper on Keisha's lap. It said, *Madame Bleu's Ballerina School* on the front. Keisha beamed from ear to ear.

1. Why did Keisha like to watch ballet?

   a. The dancers fly through the air.   b. Ballerinas wear tutus.

   c. People get to stand on their toes.   d. She wanted to be a ballerina.

2. Why did Keisha practice standing on her toes and leaping?

   _____

3. Why did Keisha ask her mom to buy her a tutu?

   _____

4. Why did Keisha cry?

   _____

5. Why did Keisha smile at the end of the story?

   _____

   _____

Look! Up in the Sky!

Answer the questions about cause and effect that follow each paragraph below.

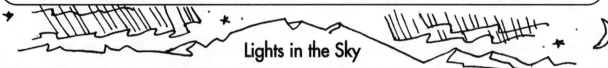

Lights in the Sky

An aurora borealis is one of the brightest night-time lights people have ever seen. It can be caused by charged particles dashing away from the sun in solar wind. It can also be caused by huge eruptions of gas on the sun called solar flares. People often describe an aurora borealis as "light dancing across the sky."

1. How many effects are discussed in this paragraph? _____

2. Explain your answer.

_____

_____

3. How many causes are discussed in this paragraph? _____

4. Explain your answer.

_____

_____

Explosion in the Sky

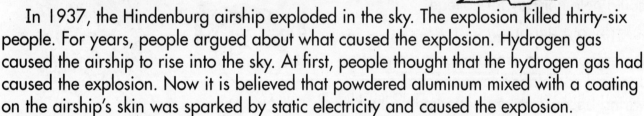

In 1937, the Hindenburg airship exploded in the sky. The explosion killed thirty-six people. For years, people argued about what caused the explosion. Hydrogen gas caused the airship to rise into the sky. At first, people thought that the hydrogen gas had caused the explosion. Now it is believed that powdered aluminum mixed with a coating on the airship's skin was sparked by static electricity and caused the explosion.

1. What did people first believe caused the explosion of the Hindenburg?

_____

_____

2. What did people later believe caused the explosion of the Hindenburg?

_____

_____

Name _____

Light the Lights!

Read the story. Then complete the activity on page 33.

Jana scrunched her nose and dove into her bed. *Not tomorrow*, she thought. She knew she'd have to give the speech she had prepared to go with her science fair project. She was terrified to speak in front of big crowds. Just thinking about the report made her heart beat faster.

Yolanda burst into Jana's room. "Did you hear," Yolanda shouted. "We could get a prize for our report tomorrow."

"What do you mean?" asked Jana.

"The City Council Science Committee is going to all the schools to listen to the reports. They're going to give a big cash prize to the people who win."

"My family could really use that money," Jana said. "Linda will be finished with high school soon, and the money could help her pay for college."

The next day, Jana and Yolanda set up the equipment to prepare for the report. Jana asked Yolanda to connect all the wiring because Yolanda worked well with electronics.

Jana opened her mouth to speak as Yolanda prepared to show the audience how the experiment worked, but not a single sound came from Jana's mouth. She felt perspiration bead up on her palms. Her hands shook. Silence filled the room.

My family needs the prize money, thought Jana. *I know I can do this.* Slowly, Jana began to speak. Her hands stopped shaking. She explained to the listeners that the lights in the experiment would light up because they received a charge from the batteries through the wiring. She explained how she and Yolanda had thought of the experiment.

The next day, Yolanda burst into Jana's room again. She was grinning from ear to ear because she was so happy. "Have you heard?" asked Yolanda. "It's the best of the best news! We won!"

"I knew we could do it," said Jana. She winked at Yolanda before she raced downstairs to tell her sister.

Light the Lights! (cont.)

Complete these sentences to show causes and effects from *Light the Lights!*

1. Jana did not even want to think about the report because...

_____

_____

2. Jana wanted to win the science competition because...

_____

_____

3. Yolanda connected the wiring because...

_____

_____

4. Jana's hands shook, and silence filled the room because...

_____

_____

5. Jana began speaking because...

_____

_____

6. The lights in the experiment lit up because...

_____

_____

7. The day after the competition, Jana raced down the stairs because...

_____

_____

Consequences

Peoples' actions cause results. For each of the story starters on pages 34–35, write a couple of sentences that show the results of the character's actions. Then write about the results of the opposite action.

1. What if Suki Forgot?

   a. Suki forgot to write her assignments in her notebook.

   _____

   _____

   b. Suki remembered to write her assignments in her notebook.

   _____

   _____

2. How Hard Did Shalti Work?

   a. Shalti wanted to be part of the school band, but he didn't practice.

   _____

   _____

   b. Shalti wanted to be part of the school band. He practiced and practiced.

   _____

   _____

   _____

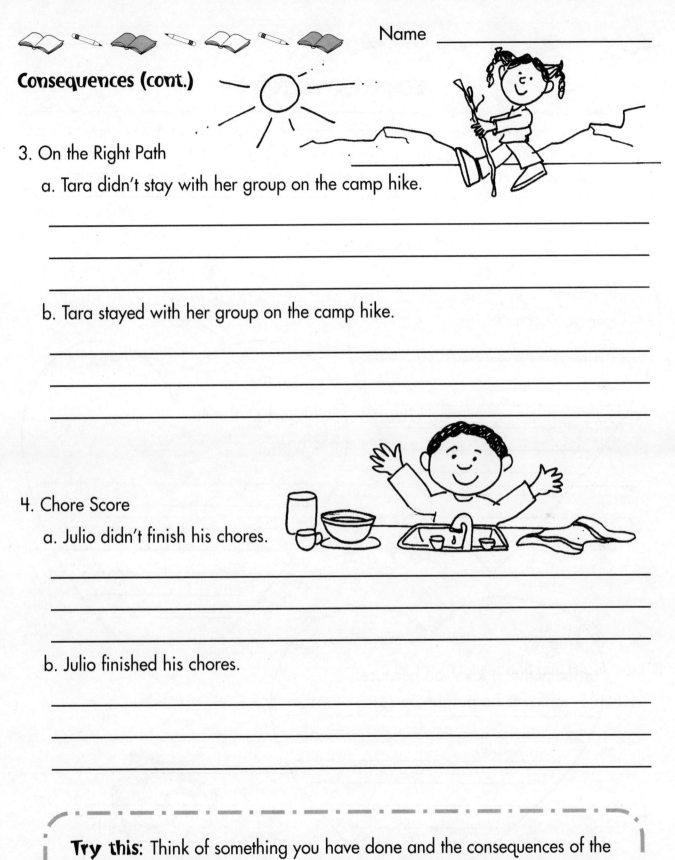

Consequences (cont.)

3. On the Right Path

   a. Tara didn't stay with her group on the camp hike.

   _____

   _____

   _____

   b. Tara stayed with her group on the camp hike.

   _____

   _____

   _____

4. Chore Score

   a. Julio didn't finish his chores.

   _____

   _____

   _____

   b. Julio finished his chores.

   _____

   _____

   _____

Try this: Think of something you have done and the consequences of the action. Write a short story that tells what would have happened if you had done the opposite.

Your New Job

You've just starting working for a greeting card company. Your work assignment is to create Valentine's Day cards. The verses on the cards must list reasons why someone is liked or loved. Write some verses for the cards. Then decorate the cards.

1. To my pet,
   I love you because...
   _____
   _____
   _____
   _____
   _____

2. To my human, I love you because...
   _____
   _____
   _____
   _____
   _____

3. To my grandmother, I love you because...
   _____
   _____
   _____
   _____
   _____

Your New Job (cont.)

4. To my sister,
   I love you
   because...

   _____
   _____
   _____
   _____
   _____

5. To my father,
   I love you because...

   _____
   _____
   _____
   _____
   _____
   _____

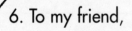

6. To my friend,
   I like you because...

   _____
   _____
   _____
   _____
   _____
   _____

Name _____

Sensible Effects

List two effects that make sense for each cause.

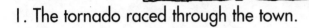

1. The tornado raced through the town.

_____

_____

2. There was no rain for two months.

_____

_____

3. The ice broke as Ahmed skated across the frozen pond.

_____

_____

4. Avishai forgot to close the birdcage door.

_____

_____

5. Sasha measured only half as much string as he needed for his science experiment.

_____

_____

6. Lena forgot to take out the trash.

_____

_____

Try this: Now write your own cause. Challenge a friend to write two effects that make sense.

Sensible Causes

List two causes that make sense for each effect.

1. The candle's flame went out.

_____

_____

2. The birds suddenly flew into the trees.

_____

_____

3. The flowers in the garden drooped.

_____

_____

4. Our dog dashed to the front door.

_____

_____

5. Our dog panted.

_____

_____

6. The boat moved across the lake.

_____

_____

Try this: Now write your own effect. Challenge a friend to write two causes that make sense.

All Arrows Point to Effect

Inside each circle, you'll find an effect. On each line pointing to the inside of the circle, write a cause that makes sense.

I received an excellent grade on my paper.

We had the best tomato crop ever.

All Arrows Point to Effect (cont.)

The class play
went very well.

The balloon floated
high in the sky.

Now write an effect of your
own inside this circle. Challenge
your classmates to think of
causes that make sense.

The Greatest Gift

Read the story. Then answer the questions on page 43.

Rena dabbed her paintbrush across her palette. She brushed the color across the canvas. *I'll never be able to do it*, she thought. She gazed at the painting on the wall of the art studio.

"Rena," said her art teacher. "What you've done here is beautiful! You have such talent. You're one of my best students because you have such an unusual style."

Rena shook her head. "Maybe, but my work will never look like that." She looked again at the painting hanging on the wall.

When Rena walked in the door at home, her little brother grabbed her by the arm. "Rena, Rena, will you make a picture for Grandpa's birthday? I wrote a poem for him, but I want to put it with a great big picture. And I want you to do it because you're such a great artist."

Rena smiled. "Okay, Oscar. Grab all those old pictures from the box."

Oscar skipped out of the room. A few minutes later, he dashed in, carrying Grandpa's photos. It was hard to piece them together because they were all torn, and they were faded, too.

At the art studio, Rena laid the torn and faded photos across a table so she could arrange them in a special way. For weeks,

Rena worked with her paints on a big canvas. She placed every stroke and chose every color with great care.

On Grandpa's birthday, Oscar read his poem. Then Rena gave Grandpa the painting. Tears filled Grandpa's eyes. "The poem was wonderful, and the painting . . . the painting shows my old friends and my old neighborhood in a way that makes me feel as though I'm there all over again. Rena you've shown me how special all these people have been in my life. You and Oscar are wonderful."

The Greatest Gift (cont.)

> Answer these cause and effect questions about *The Greatest Gift*.

1. Why did Rena's art teacher like Rena's work?

_____

_____

_____

2. Why did Oscar want Rena to paint a picture for Grandpa?

_____

_____

_____

3. Why was it hard to piece together Grandpa's old photos?

_____

_____

_____

4. Why did Grandpa cry when he saw Rena's painting?

_____

_____

_____

Try this: Think of something nice you can do for a friend or family member and do it.

The Giant Wave

Read the article. Then complete the sentences to tell causes and effects from *The Giant Wave*.

You have probably heard about earthquakes. Earthquakes are caused by a trembling of the earth's crust. Earthquakes occur mostly because big pieces of the earth's crust rub against each other. As exciting as earthquakes are, you may never have heard about *tsunamis*. Japan experiences a tsunami at least once every few years.

A tsunami is a gargantuan wave caused by underwater earthquakes, landslides, or volcanoes. The moving of the earth's crust under the water creates huge amounts of damage, much like an earthquake on dry land. A tsunami can reach heights of 100 feet (31 m)!

Because tsunami experts want to save lives and property, they have created the Pacific Tsunami Warning System. This system works by finding earthquakes that may cause a tsunami. This warning system helps people seek safety when a tsunami is going to hit Japan.

1. Earthquakes and tsunamis are both caused by...

_____

_____

2. A tsunami causes...

_____

_____

3. Experts have created a warning system because...

_____

_____

4. The warning system helps people because...

_____

_____

WELCOME TO NIAGARA

Washed Away

Read the article. Then answer the questions below.

Erosion causes rocks and soil to be broken down. It can be caused by water, wind, ice, or gravity. People often think of erosion by water because it can be so noticable. One famous example of erosion is Niagara Falls. These falls used to be 7 miles (11 km) away from their current position but have moved over the years because of erosion. Water and small pieces of rock have worn away the cliffs and caused the flow of water to slowly move backward. Because some of the rock is softer, it is worn away first. If you were to take all the water away from the falls, you would see that the top of the rock sticks out farther than the bottom. This is because the bottom rock is softer.

Erosion is always at work. The more water that flows over rocks, the more the rocks erode. At Niagara Falls, they have tried to slow down the erosion by stopping some of the water from reaching the falls. So, only some of the water that should be eroding the rock is doing its job. However, the falls will still continue to slowly erode. People can try to slow down erosion, but they will never stop it.

1. Why have the Niagara Falls moved?

_____

_____

2. Why does the top of Niagara Falls stick out farther than the bottom?

_____

_____

3. Why have people tried to stop water from going over the falls?

_____

_____

4. What do you think will eventually happen to Niagara Falls?

_____

_____

1. b
2. d
3. a
4. c

Students' written answers will vary but should show an understanding of cause and effect.

Inside camp cabin: she loves tennis classes, people are nice, she likes riding horses

Inside apartment building: she misses her own tennis court, she misses her grandma and their tennis matches, food is better at home, she misses frozen yogurt

1. d
2. b
3. f
4. a
5. c
6. g
7. e

1. g
2. d
3. b
4. h
5. c
6. e
7. a
8. f

1. c
2. b
3. a
4. b
5. a

1. e
2. a
3. f
4. d
5. c
6. b

Butterfly Bushes:
1. José's garden must have plants caterpillars like.
2. José's garden must have plants butterflies like.

Delilah's Delight:
1. Pesticides can be bad for the environment.
2. Ladybugs munch insect pests.

Creature Feature:
1. Crickets look for mates.
2. Scout bees find lots of food.

Student paragraphs will vary but should show an understanding of cause and effect sentences.

Answers will vary. Possible answers are:
1. The boy is grabbing his raincoat because it is raining.

2. The dog is thirsty because there is no water in its dish.
3. The boy missed the bus because he was late.

Student pictures and sentences will vary but should show an understanding of cause and effect.

1. **cause:** Because of oil spills, **effect:** many sea creatures have died.
2. **cause:** because some people have failed to properly dispose of waste. **effect:** Ducks have been found with plastic drink rings around their necks
3. **cause:** Since turtles are often harmed by traps, **effect:** many kinds of traps have been outlawed.
4. **cause:** For protection, **effect:** lobsters walk in single file when they migrate.
5. **cause:** so that the ray can get the food it needs. **effect:** A manta ray's gills filter plankton from the water,
6. **cause:** Because killer whales eat fish and small mammals, **effect:** they have cone-shaped teeth that help them chew their prey.
7. **cause:** Because redfish were endangered, **effect:** fishing for redfish was

not permitted.

Rhyme Climb..............................16–17

Cause

1. Simple Simon had no money.
2. The cow jumped over the moon.

Effect

3. It frightened Miss Muffet away.
4. Little Johnny wants the rain to go away.

Dressing for Dinner..............................18–19

Student letters should reflect that Will mixed up the quantities of oil and vinegar.

Because I'll Be Responsible..............................20–21

1. Josh had not taken care of his hamster.
2. He felt sad and disappointed.
3. He wanted to prove that he could be responsible.
4. Josh had proven that he could be responsible.

Proverbial Cause..............................22–23

Answers will vary. Possible answers are:

2. One final small problem can cause people big problems.
3. Don't count on something before you actually have it because you could be disappointed.
4. You shouldn't make assumptions based on appearance.
5. A busy person advances in a positive way.
6. Don't waste time worrying

about the past, because you can spend time making the present better.

Science Action..............................24–25

1. c
2. c
3. a
4. b

Cause Pause..............................26

1. was as red as a lobster.
2. got a huge blister on my heel.
3. felt a tug at the end of the line.
4. fell backwards as all the pieces spilled across the floor.
5. twisted my ankle.

Speaker Squeaker..............................27

1. The bright sun shone right in my eyes.
2. Mom touched the match to the candle.
3. We watered the garden every day.
4. I pedaled my bike as hard as I could.
5. I kicked with all my might.

How the World Wide Web Came to Be..............................28

1. He wanted to create a way to organize and find information.
2. They needed to come up with a name quickly.
3. Answers will vary.

Out-of-This-World Vacation..............................29

1. People love thrills and fun.
2. There is no gravity.
3. The travelers will be high

above the earth.

4. There is not very much fresh air.
5. They will need life insurance.
6. Fuel costs are high.

A Grand Debut..............................30

1. a
2. She wanted to be a ballerina.
3. She was desperate.
4. She wasn't a ballerina.
5. She will go to ballet school.

Look! Up in the Sky!..............................31

Lights in the Sky

1. one
2. The aurora borealis is the main effect.
3. two
4. The aurora borealis is caused by charged bits dashing away from the sun in solar wind or by huge eruptions of gas called solar flares.

Explosion in the Sky

1. They first believed that hydrogen gas caused the explosion.
2. They later believed that powdered aluminum mixed with a coating on the airship's skin caused the explosion.

Light the Lights!..............................32–33

1. she was terrified to speak in front of crowds.
2. her family needed the money.
3. she worked well with electronics.
4. she was afraid to speak.
5. she knew her family needed

the money; she overcame her fear.

6. they received a charge from the batteries through the wiring.

7. she was happy and wanted to tell her sister.

Answers will vary, but should show an understanding of consequences.

Answers will vary but should show an understanding of cause and effect.

Answers will vary. Possible answers are:

1. Buildings were destroyed. Tree limbs were all over the street.
2. People could not water their lawns. Fish didn't have enough water in lakes.
3. Ahmed fell through the ice. Ahmed quickly skated off the pond.
4. The bird flew out. The bird got lost.
5. The experiment result was incorrect. Sasha could not complete the experiment.
6. The trash smelled bad. Lena had twice as much trash to take out the following week.

Answers will vary. Possible

answers are:

1. The wind blew. Someone blew on the flame.
2. A cat ran into the yard. There was a loud banging noise.
3. There was no rain. We forgot to water them.
4. The doorbell rang. Mom drove in the driveway.
5. It was hot outside. The dog had just run through the yard.
6. The wind filled its sails. People rowed the boat.

Answers will vary but should show an understanding of cause and effect and consequences of actions.

1. She had an unusual style.
2. He wanted to give it to Grandpa for his birthday.
3. The photos were torn and faded.
4. Her painting brought the past back to him and showed him how special many people had been in his life.

1. the earth's crust moving.
2. huge amounts of damage.
3. they want to save lives and property.
4. they can seek safety.

1. Water and rock have worn

away the cliffs.

2. The rock on the bottom is softer and wears away first.
3. They want to slow down erosion
4. Answers will vary.